Asun Balzola
Josep M. Parramón

Spring

CHILDRENS PRESS, CHICAGO
School & Library Edition
ISBN 0-516-02381-0

When the apple trees bud...

... and
the fields
are green...

... and the plants
grow

and the flowers
bloom!

When the sky
is blue

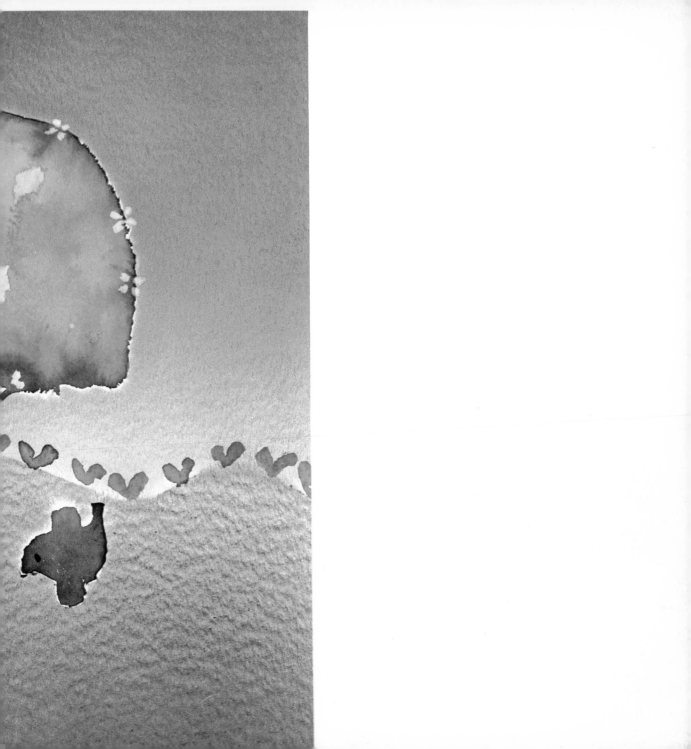

... and houses
look bright...

When the
birds
fly north

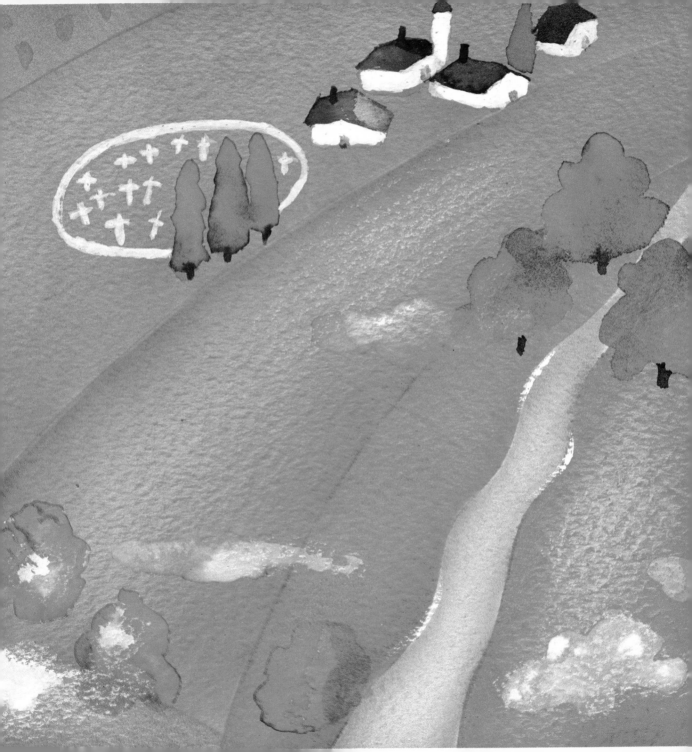

... and butterflies
take wing...

When love
is born again

and the sun warms...

and
children play...

It's spring!

SPRING

Fruit trees bud

On the branches of the apple tree small white and pink blossoms appear. Spring has come! Months later, in October, when summer is over, the blossoms will have become ripe apples ready to be made into pies and cakes and candy apples.

Plants grow and flowers bloom.

Why is it that in spring the fields become green again, the plants grow, buds burst, and flowers bloom?

It is because the snow on the mountains has melted, rivers and brooks run over their banks and the sun comes closer to the earth and warms the plants. But above all, it is because spring is a time of rain.

Sun, rain and wind in April and May.

The farmer knows this is what must happen. The rest of the year depends on April and May. Sun and rain during these months bring a rich harvest in July, August and September.
And the wind? Why the wind?

What does the wind do?

The wind alternates rain and sun and now and then sweeps the clouds from the sky and leaves it blue. The wind also blows the seeds to the ground and pollen from flower to flower so things can grow. This is how the plants grow, the fields turn green, and the flowers bloom!

The birds fly north.

This is another sign of spring: the return of the birds. In March millions of birds fly north, build nests, lay eggs, and start new families. Then in the fall, when the weather turns cold, they return south.

Spring and love.

Spring is nature's triumph: It brings us flowers, birds, baby animals, parties, Easter, Passover... It is not only by chance that the blood moves faster in spring and that May is the month of flowers.

E
Pa

Parramon, Josep M
Spring.

Buhl Public Library

1. The borrower is responsible for all books drawn on his card and for fines on his overdue books.

2. A fine of 2 cents a day will be charged on each book which is not returned on or by the date stamped.

DEMCO